Original title:
Finding Purpose Through the Chaos

Copyright © 2025 Creative Arts Management OÜ
All rights reserved.

Author: Rosalie Bradford
ISBN HARDBACK: 978-1-80566-194-8
ISBN PAPERBACK: 978-1-80566-489-5

The Alchemy of Life

In the circus of life, I juggle my socks,
While pondering if pizza counts as detox.
The coffee spills jump, like they want to dance,
Every morning's a bungle, but hey, there's a chance!

With chaos around me, I plot my grand scheme,
A quest for lost keys and whipped cream supreme.
My blender's a wizard, it whirs and it hums,
While I try to find sense in the rattle of drums.

I chase after dreams like a cat on a kite,
They swirl in the air, oh what a silly sight!
I trip on my thoughts, then I giggle and glide,
In this jumble of joy, there's nowhere to hide.

So I dance with the madness, let laughter take flight,
In the chaos and clatter, I find my delight.
For life's a great mix, like socks in the wash,
Just embrace all the whirls, and give fate a nudge!

Seasons of Rediscovery

In spring I lost my favorite shoe,
A squirrel wore it, who knew?
Summer sun made me reconsider,
Chasing shadows, feeling bitter.

Autumn leaves danced like my lost keys,
I tripped and fell with graceful ease.
Winter came with a frosty glare,
Don't forget to breathe that crisp air!

Glimmers in Darkness

Late-night snacks, the fridge is bare,
Stumbling, I find a yogurt there.
Illuminated by the fridge light's glow,
I ponder what I really know.

The cat laughs at my midnight quest,
He's living proof of the best jest.
In the chaos of my hungry plight,
I twirl and dance in the moonlight!

The Thread of Existence

I knit with yarn, a tangled mess,
Each stitch I make is pure distress.
But like toasts given at a wedding,
I find humor in this threading.

A scarf that grows a foot each day,
A fashion statement that's here to stay.
In the fibers of life, I strive and glow,
Each knot a giggle, a tale to show!

Dancing with the Storm

Raindrops tap a merry beat,
I slip and slide on my own two feet.
Lightning flashes, almost shouts,
"Come join this dance, let go of doubts!"

Umbrellas flip like comments made,
In this chaos, joy won't fade.
Clumsy twirls, a splash or two,
Together we jive, just me and you!

When Silence Speaks

In the quiet, chaos whirls,
A cat named Whiskers twirls.
He claims he's wise and full of flair,
Yet knocks over my favorite chair.

In the stillness, laughter sings,
A sock puppet pulls invisible strings.
Whispers of mischief fill the air,
As I dance with my lunch—who needs a care?

When silence tries to set the mood,
I find my sock drawer in a feud.
As chaos reigns with silly grace,
I'm laughing at the messy space.

The Beauty of Brokenness

A vase once grand, now on the floor,
Yet flowers bloom like never before.
Cracks and chips like tales untold,
Each shard a moment, brave and bold.

In the chaos, we see the glow,
A squirrel who thinks he runs the show.
With acorns dropping, all around,
Each scatter brings a joyful sound.

Broken things can't take the heat,
Yet still, they find a way to greet.
With every laugh and little mess,
We find beauty in our strange distress.

Rediscovering Light

In the dark, I trip and pout,
Yet a glowbug's dance brings me about.
He flits and giggles in my ear,
"Step lightly now, the fun is near!"

With shadows thrown like cheeseballs wide,
I laugh at myself, with arms open wide.
Cracks in the walls let in the sun,
As we find joy in laughter, oh what fun!

Underneath the chaos' glare,
A playful heart finds sweet repair.
For in each stumble, laughter's bright,
We rediscover warmth and light.

The Heart's Resilience

My heart once locked in a rusty cage,
Now dances joyfully on a stage.
With quirky moves, it shimmies free,
As I trip on my own two feet!

With each mishap, I twirl and spin,
Bumping into walls, but I just grin.
A rubber chicken comes to play,
Making wins out of disarray.

Chaos gives a nudge or two,
Where lemons grow in shades of blue.
Resilient hearts just chuckle and say,
"Breakdowns can be a fun buffet!"

In the Heart of the Whirlwind

In a tornado of socks and old receipts,
I dance like no one's watching my clumsy feats.
Coffee spills and cat hair flies,
I'm a circus act with a side of fries.

Chasing deadlines like a bird on a spree,
I trip on my own two feet, oh woe is me!
But amidst the chaos, I wear a grin,
For laughter's the prize that I hope to win.

Sunrays Through the Cracks

A coffee cup in one hand, a cat in the other,
Juggling my life like some overgrown mother.
Sunbeams sneak through, lighting up my mess,
I laugh at my chaos, it's hard to impress!

Dishes stack high like a treacherous game,
Yet here I am smiling, it's hard to feel shame.
With every spill and the whir of the broom,
I'm the queen of this castle, chaos blooms.

Calm Within the Roar

In the midst of the uproar—oh what a show!
The alarm clocks are screaming, the kids' faces glow.
Yet, here I am sipping my tea with a grin,
Wrapped in the madness, oh let the fun begin!

The dog's barking loudly, the world's gone askew,
But I'll be the captain of this zany zoo.
With chaos my compass, I'll navigate snide,
Finding joy in the jumbles of life far and wide.

The Unexpected Path in the Wilderness

Lost in the woods where the wild things trod,
I trip over roots and laugh at the odd.
Mushrooms are plotted like some grand parade,
Who knew hiking felt more like a charade?

Brushing off leaves while searching for signs,
I'm an explorer with no grand designs.
Yet through the snags and the rips in my pants,
I find that life's trouble is just one big dance!

Sculpting Meaning

In a world of mashed potatoes,
I seek a sculptor's clay.
With every twist of fate's fork,
I chip my worries away.

Life tosses pies in the air,
And I dance to their flight.
Catch one, you might just trip—
A slapstick show at night.

With chaos at every turn,
I juggle my lost dreams.
A circus clown with visions,
Laughter bursts at the seams.

So here's to misfit moments,
Where giggles sneak on through.
With a wink and a leap,
In chaos, I find my view.

Navigating Life's Tides

I'm a captain on a raft,
Rowing with a broomstick.
The waves are mischief makers,
And my compass, rather slick.

Flip-flops on the ocean,
A pirate made of foam.
Swapping out my treasure maps,
For snacks and a warm dome.

The tide pulls me this way,
Then flings me on that side.
I'm just a bobbing buoy,
And the sea's my silly ride.

Laughter splashes with the waves,
As I paddle through the strife.
In every twist of humor,
I find this wobbly life.

The Space Between

In the space between my thoughts,
A squirrel wears a tie.
He's planning his next business move,
On a branch, oh so spry.

I juggle all my worries,
Like hot potatoes tossed.
Every thought, a bouncing ball,
With giggles, I feel lost.

In this limbo dance, I sway,
Mixing joy with my dread.
Still, I pluck the wisest fruit,
From the chaos in my head.

So raise a cup of tea with me,
In this wacky floaty scene.
For in the space between the jests,
Life's nonsense reigns supreme.

Dance of Uncertainty

In the ballroom of question marks,
I stumble on my feet.
Two left shoes and a wild hat,
Make this dance quite a treat.

The music's a lively riddle,
With twists that leave me spun.
But I twirl through tangled answers,
And still have so much fun.

Each slip a new adventure,
In this wobbly ballet.
With laughter at each misstep,
I twist chaos into play.

So let's embrace the funky beats,
Of this odd, bewildering chance.
In the dance of my confusion,
I find my rhythm and prance.

Unseen Pathways

With socks on the ceiling, I chart my way,
Through tumbledown treasures where oddities play.
Spilled cereal whispers, a laughter-filled guide,
In a world of wild wonders, I take a wild ride.

An umbrella in sunlight? A hat on my cat,
Confetti of choices, a curious spat.
Each twist of the journey, a joke to unravel,
In this blessed chaos, I skip and I travel.

Balancing on the Edge

I walk on a tightrope made of spaghetti,
Juggling two thoughts but my mind's feeling petty.
A duck in a top hat quacks, "Life's quite absurd!"
As I search for my balance, I slip on a word.

A dance in my kitchen, I slide across tiles,
With cereal boxes, I craft funny piles.
The world spins around me, a topsy-turvy show,
But laughter's my anchor, and off I go!

The Clarity in Chaos

In the midst of the whirlwind, I wear mismatched shoes,
Searching for answers in the overly caffeinated blues.
A cat in a tutu prances, showing the way,
While life throws me curveballs, I twist, sway, and play.

A blender of dreams whirls with noisy delight,
As I chase down my thoughts that sprint out of sight.
With pancakes for wisdom and syrup for cheer,
I dance through confusion—no need to adhere.

Raindrops of Realization

Raindrops are tickling my nose in a rush,
Umbrellas are dancing, all in a big crush.
As puddles plot parties beneath my two feet,
I find inspiration in chaos, so sweet.

A rubber duck sails on the lake of my mind,
While lightning bolts giggle, oh how they're unkind!
With whims and with wiggles, I splash in the rain,
Discovering joy when I'm soaked to the brain.

Purpose in the Aftermath

In a world where socks do flee,
I chase them like a bumblebee.
With a smile that's plastered wide,
I wear my laundry like it's pride.

My cereal's a masterpiece,
A splash of chaos, pure caprice.
I laugh as milk spills on the floor,
Decorating the kitchen door.

Life's a puzzle, pieces missed,
Like a cat on a lawyer's list.
Yet I dance with mismatched shoes,
Embracing all the silly blues.

The Labyrinth's Embrace

In a maze of lost TV remotes,
I wander like bewildered goats.
Chasing whims and coffee stains,
Life's a circus with no reins.

The GPS is mocking me,
With turnarounds of comedy.
I take a left, and then a right,
Ending up where there's no light.

Yet in this wild, topsy-turvy game,
I find my spark and light the flame.
With every twist, a chuckle stays,
I steer through life's bizarre ballet.

Unruly Grace

Balancing books on my head,
While juggling eggs that might be dead.
I twirl around the pizza box,
Embracing chaos—who needs clocks?

My cat's the boss, it's true, you see,
She reigns the piles of laundry, free.
With every nap and pouncing spree,
She teaches me to just be me.

I stomp on Lego, yelp and sing,
In painful zeal, I learn this thing.
Through clumsy moves, I find my way,
In wild missteps, I seize the day.

Beneath the Surface

Underneath my coffee's lace,
A whirlpool brews, a frumpy race.
I splash and giggle, spill my fate,
In caffeine chaos, I celebrate.

The dishes tower like a game,
But I just laugh, it's all the same.
With spoons and forks, I carve a path,
To find the joy in quirky math.

Underneath the piles of clothes,
I dance and frolic, who even knows?
With tangled threads, my heart's a song,
In every clash, I still belong.

Blooming Amidst the Ruins

In a garden of socks, I trip and I fall,
Laughter erupts, hear my clumsy call.
Weeds sprout like dreams that can't be ignored,
Amidst broken pots, my humor's restored.

A cat's on the table, a dog on my knee,
Juggling the chaos, still sipping my tea.
Life's messy and wild, but that's just my style,
Embracing the madness, I can still smile.

Dancing with dust bunnies, I run from despair,
With fuzzy green friends, I float through the air.
Each slip and each tumble, a step towards the bright,
In life's tangled garden, I find my delight.

So hand me a shovel, let's dig for the fun,
In the ruins of laughter, I'm never outrun.
Blooming with giggles, my spirit takes flight,
In my own happy chaos, everything's right.

Fragments of Serenity

Coffee spills over, splashing the floor,
A rude little wake-up, my morning's uproar.
With crumbs on my shirt and a sock in my hair,
I ponder my life while I'm stuck in this chair.

The cat is a judge, my thoughts on display,
Critiquing my choices in a feline ballet.
With attitude fierce, she makes her decree,
"Just roll with the punches, it's funnier, see?"

A puzzle half-solved, with pieces askew,
Like life, it's a jumble of shades dark and blue.
Yet somewhere in chaos, I find a sweet rhyme,
Fragments of laughter that dance through the grime.

In puddles of nonsense, I wade with a grin,
Serenity's echoes begin from within.
So cheers to the chaos, the giggles it brings,
In fragments of madness, I've grown my own wings.

The Compass Within

In a world that spins like a top on the run,
I've lost my directions, but found some fun.
With laughter my compass, I wade through the day,
Navigating chaos in my own silly way.

I followed a squirrel to map out my fate,
It danced on the pavement, a cute little mate.
With acorns for wisdom and nutty delight,
My compass points straight to a whimsical night.

Each wrong turn I take is a giggle in disguise,
Guided by chuckles that spark in my eyes.
Through tumble and jangle, I'm learning to see,
That the heart of the chaos is laughter's decree.

So here's to the journey, no map to confine,
With joy as my compass, my spirit can shine.
In this wild adventure, I'll spin and I'll twirl,
Finding treasure in laughter, in this topsy-turvy world.

Stars in the Tempest

When storms come a-knocking, my hair starts to frizz,
I slip on a banana peel, just like that fizz.
But in each wild tempest, I find a bright star,
With giggles and chaos, I've come oh so far.

The wind roars like laughter, it shakes up my plans,
Dancing in puddles while twisting my pants.
The clouds may be frowning, but I'm shooting for joy,
In storms filled with chuckles, my heart's a buoy.

With umbrellas like boats, I soar through the breeze,
My compass is giggles, my spirit's at ease.
So let the rain drench me, I'll splash with a grin,
In the stars of the storm, I find what's within.

So I raise my umbrella, a toast to the night,
To chaos and stars, to the wild, the bright.
In the tempest of laughter, my heart's so alive,
It's in all of this chaos where I truly thrive.

Fragments of Light in a Darkened World

In the mess of socks and dreams,
I trip on my own schemes.
A cat jumps high, knocks tea away,
as I laugh at a brand new day.

Cooking chaos fills the air,
a pepper dance, my culinary flare.
The smoke alarm sings a song,
while I sing along, nothing feels wrong.

My plants are all in disarray,
yet somehow they bloom today.
A flower peeks from leafy sprawl,
as I ponder, can I keep it all?

Juggling tasks like wobbly clowns,
while my laundry piles like mountain towns.
But amidst the whirl of daily strife,
moments shine like a comical life.

The Resilient Flame in the Gale.

A candle flickers in the breeze,
it dances wild with silly ease.
Its wax drips down in crazy lanes,
but hey, at least it still remains!

The world spins fast, enough to annoy,
yet I craft laughter, my secret joy.
I trip and tumble, land on my face,
how do I life with such grace?

With a coffee cup held like a prize,
I watch my plants grow in disguise.
Their leaves are bent and full of glee,
in this quirky little world of me.

Through gales that try to blow me away,
I find my spark in the disarray.
And as I bumble, giggling loud,
these tiny flames create a crowd.

Whispers in the Turmoil

In chaos, whispers softly bloom,
a pet goldfish finds a broom.
I spill my thoughts like marbles round,
and search for silence in the sound.

The coffee brews like a wild beast,
its aroma claims my heart, at least.
I wear my shirt back to front,
the day's begun, quite the jaunt!

The schedule's a jigsaw, missing pieces,
while laughter bubbles and never ceases.
I chase my keys, they're on a spree,
a squirrel steals the show from me!

Yet in all this goofy, mad charade,
I find the beauty time has made.
With every laugh, a purpose spins,
turns chaos into joyful grins.

The Art of Rebirth

With glitter stuck upon my nose,
I'm crafting art in silly prose.
My paintbrush slips, the canvas sighs,
while I create with woeful cries.

A seed I planted yesterday,
turns into weeds that sing and sway.
Yet in these greens, I find my song,
for chaos brings me where I belong.

I lose my keys, not once but twice,
and paint my thoughts, oh so precise.
Each project fails in an awkward dance,
yet somehow, I give life another chance.

And as I navigate this wild art,
a quirky smile warms my heart.
Through slips and trips, a tale unfolds,
in chaos, new adventure molds.

Threads of Destiny

In a world that spins with threads so thin,
I trip on my shoelaces but still begin.
The fabric of life's a patchwork quilt,
With cotton candy dreams and a sprinkle of guilt.

I tried to sew straight, but I stitched in a twist,
Patterns emerge that I never wished.
Dancing with fate, I trip on my toes,
But laughter's the thread that forever flows.

Some call it chaos, I call it a game,
With popcorn for problems, I'll stake my claim.
The needle's sharp, but my heart is a joke,
Stitch it all up and watch how we poke.

Amid all the fibers, I find pure delight,
Even tangled in yarn, I still feel so light.
So I gather my threads, let them twirl and spin,
In this colorful mess, I feel like a win.

Starlight Through Cracks

In the cracks of my world, light flickers so bright,
Like rogue fireflies crashing my quirky night.
I sway to the rhythm of misfit beats,
Chasing down starlight with wobbly feet.

The universe laughs as I tumble and roll,
Collecting all dreams like a scavenger's scroll.
With a wink from the cosmos and a wink from a cat,
I ponder if chaos is where happiness sat.

Cracks in reality let the laughter in,
Each chuckle a spark, igniting my grin.
The more that I stumble, the more that I soar,
Breathing stardust and giggles, who could want more?

So come join my dance under shimmering sway,
In the cracks of existence, we'll wiggle and play.
Together we'll find in the mayhem a spark,
A humorous journey ignited in dark.

Finding Harmony in Discord

In a world full of noise, I'm the loudest sound,
Like a rogue kazoo in a symphony found.
My life's a tune played by a clumsy old band,
Where harmony's lost but still oh so grand.

I skip on the keys that are slightly offbeat,
With a tap dance of chaos, I lift up my feet.
Discord is music; it plays in my veins,
Each hiccup a note that joyously reigns.

Some think I'm a clown, but I'm just bizarre,
Riding the chaos like a shiny blue car.
As laughter erupts from the snafu I face,
I weave through the dissonance, finding my place.

So bring on the chaos, I'll play my own way,
Through the laughs and the giggles, I'll dance and I'll sway.
In the symphony silly, I know I belong,
With a wink to the mess, I compose my own song.

Rising from the Ashes

Like a phoenix who snoozed in a pile of hot coals,
I wake up confused, with marvelous goals.
In flames of mishaps, I've made quite a scene,
Dancing in embers, oh what could have been!

With a hairdryer in hand, I'm fanning the spark,
Kicking up dust like I'm running a lark.
Each fiery flub is a lesson, no doubt,
When chaos is king, I can't live without!

I trip over ashes, I stumble and laugh,
Each misadventure, my comic craft.
So here's to my ashes, they're fluffy and grand,
Creating a castle of chaos I planned.

From the depths of the weird, I rise up with glee,
Like a jester in flames, wild and carefree.
So let's toast to the journey, the chaos, the fun,
In this wacky adventure, we've only begun!

In the Eye of the Storm

A cat on a roof, defying the rain,
Chasing its tail, ignores all the pain.
Dancing in droplets, like a quirky ballet,
Who knew chaos could bring out such play?

The winds are a whirl, a wild serenade,
Yet here I am, perfectly made.
With socks on my hands, I strut down the street,
Laughing at life as it slips off its seat.

Lightning strikes twice, but I'm holding my ground,
Juggling life's lemons, it's chaos abound!
But hey, there's a rainbow, I swear it's not shy,
Guess I'll bake pancakes while the storm passes by.

In storms that perplex, I wear my odd hat,
With gumboots and giggles, I'm where I'm at.
So here's to the chaos, let's give it a whirl,
For even in madness, I can still give a twirl.

Serenity's Echo

In a world full of mess, I brew my sweet tea,
With crumbs on my shirt, I just let it be.
The cat finds my lap a perfect new throne,
While I ponder my life, with cheese on my bone.

I step on a Lego, a painful rude joke,
Yet laughter ignites, I'm chuckling, not broke.
For every disaster, there's humor to find,
Like socks in the dryer that vanish, unkind.

My plants are all wilting, they crave a good feed,
I wonder if coffee could replace all their needs?
Yet in this mad garden, a dandelion smiles,
As I sip on my chaos and laugh for a while.

Though life's like a circus, I'm still in the seat,
With clowns and confusion, I'm dancing to beat.
So here's to the chaos, let's lift up a cheer,
In this wild serenade, I've got nothing to fear.

The Symphony of Struggle

With pots on my head, I dance in the rain,
Stirring up mischief, embracing the pain.
Is that music I hear? Or just my old dog?
He's jamming along in the thick of the fog.

My life's like a symphony, slightly off-key,
With trumpets and trombones just playing for me.
Though the rhythm is weird, and the tempo's a mess,
My heart's got a beat that no chaos can stress.

Tangled up wires, my headphones a fright,
But I'll crank up the volume and dance through the night.
With spoons and a broomstick, I'll lead this parade,
In the orchestra of life, a grand serenade.

Each mishap a note, in my chaotic score,
Yet laughter and joy build the tempo even more.
So here's to the struggles, let's laugh through the strife,
In the wild symphony, I'm living my life.

Glistening Amidst Grime

In my messy kitchen, I'm cooking up dreams,
With flour on my face, it's bursting at the seams.
Dishes piled high, a tower of fun,
But who needs a clean plate when you've got a pun?

The floors might be sticky, but I'll slide with grace,
As I dance with the mop, at a very slow pace.
Life's like a pizza, deliciously odd,
And I'm just the chef with a cheeky façade.

In the chaos of crumbs, I'll whistle a tune,
As my cat sneaks a nibble, and things go kaboom!
Yet amid all the mess, there's magic to find,
With laughter that sparkles, and joy intertwined.

So here's to the grime, the gooey delight,
For in every big mess, there's a moment that's bright.
With scissors and giggles, I'll craft my own glee,
In this glorious chaos, just let me be me.

Mapping Stars in a Cloudy Night

In clouds of cotton candy fluff,
We squint at stars, there's not enough.
The map is crazy, drawn in crayon,
But hey, at least we've got a crayon!

Chasing wishes on a bumpy ride,
With lollipops and giggles, side by side.
We stomp the puddles, make a splash,
While wishing life would go a bit more brash.

A compass spins like a whirling dervish,
Yet here we are, feeling quite swedish.
Who needs directions, or even a plan?
Let's doodle our fate like a happy fan!

On this wild ride of squishy delight,
We'll dance through the chaos, hearts alight.
With every twirl, the stars come back clear,
In a cloud of laughter, we'll have no fear!

Serenity's Song in a Fractured World

In a world that's turned upside down,
We wear our smiles like a shiny crown.
The streets are bumpy, and so are the trails,
But watch us dance, in our silly flails!

With socks that don't match, and hair in a mess,
We strut through chaos, we couldn't care less.
A serenade of laughter, with a twist of fate,
We sing off-key, but it feels just great!

With yogurt smears and coffee spills,
Every hiccup adds to our zany thrills.
A fractured world can be quite a show,
With giggles and wiggles, we steal the glow!

So in this ruckus, let's play and play,
With nonsense moments that chase blues away.
We'll find our harmony, each note a surprise,
In this fractured tale, we'll help each other rise!

Unraveling the Knots of Chaos

Tangled headphones in a pile of glee,
Like life's little puzzles, just wait and see!
We tug and pull, then laugh out loud,
At the mess we made of our own little crowd.

With socks that vanish and keys that hide,
We wander aimless, with chaos as our guide.
A jumbled heart beats in a wild dance,
In this circus of life, we'll take our chance!

Each twist and knot a reason to smile,
Through tangled tales, let's stay a while.
Life's a knotty string, but we'll braid it right,
With chuckles and hugs, we'll shine our light!

So here we go, in this haphazard game,
With every slip-up, we'll stake our claim.
Unraveled yet whole, we'll cheer and toast,
To our knotted adventures, we'll laugh the most!

The Quiet Strength in Whirlwinds

In the eye of the storm, there's a twirling bliss,
Like a dog in circles, it's hard to miss.
With pizza slices flying through the air,
We giggle and whirl without a care!

The world spins wildly, but we stand tall,
With bubblegum strength, we won't fall.
Like juggling clowns, we toss about,
In our funny frenzy, there's never a doubt!

A whirlwind of chaos, but here we sip tea,
With cookies and laughter, just you and me.
The quiet within is a bold serenade,
As we dance in the chaos, unafraid!

So grab your capes, let's run in the breeze,
With whispers of strength, we'll do as we please.
Through the storms of life, we'll shine like the sun,
In this whirl of wonder, we've already won!

A Journey Through Turbulence

In a world where socks go missing,
And my cat thinks she's a queen,
I tripped over my cluttered thoughts,
Yet laughter is always seen.

I spilled coffee on my to-do,
It's now an abstract art,
The chaos spins like a cartoon,
Where each mishap's a new start.

I searched for answers in the fridge,
"Knowing or cheese?" I mused,
But life's unpredictable dance,
Is the magic I've chosen to fuse.

So here I am, a jester king,
Wielding joy like a bright sword,
In the mess and the madness I sing,
Each blunder, a funny reward.

Seeds of Intention

Planted my goals in the garden,
Next to carrots dressed in blue,
The weeds say, "You'll never make it!"
I told them, "Just watch what I do!"

I watered dreams with silly songs,
And danced in the rain with flair,
The squirrels laughed at my silly moves,
But I just twirled without a care.

The daisies winked, the tulips grinned,
As I made plans with a gopher,
I asked him, "What's your secret to joy?"
He chuckled, "Life's a goofy offer."

So in chaos, I plant my seeds,
Among the laughter and cheer,
With dirt on my hands and joy in my heart,
I'm blooming right here, oh dear!

The Map of Stillness

I found a map inside my drawer,
It led to nowhere, or maybe,
A place where socks don't fight their pairs,
And calm reigns like a cuddly baby.

X marks the spot of my lost car keys,
Sipping tea while chaos reigned,
I sketched a route with doodles and laughs,
Where sanity might be regained.

The compass spun, it pointed south,
I followed the laughter we made,
In the stillness of pure nonsense,
I realized joy's never delayed.

My map's a whimsical riddle,
A treasure hunt full of cheer,
So, let's venture where chaos calls,
For laughter is always near.

Transforming Shadows

Shadows dance like old clowns,
Making faces on the wall,
They whisper stories of mishaps,
As I chase them with a sprawl.

I turned on the light, ready to boast,
But the shadows just rolled their eyes,
"Your troubles are just a funny coat!"
They giggled, in a humorized guise.

I juggled fears like ripe tomatoes,
Eating breadcrumbs of my dreams,
Every slip a reason to cackle,
As life plays its silly schemes.

So let's toast to the night and its quirks,
To the fun in our little flops,
For in the dance of transforming shadows,
We find joy, and the laughter never stops.

The Whisper of Purpose

In the jumble of socks and lost keys,
I laugh at the chaos with such ease.
A donut in hand, I ponder and float,
Dancing with dreams, on a tiny toy boat.

Mismatched shoes on a wobbly line,
I trip on my thoughts, but I'm feelin' fine.
A squirrel steals my lunch, what a cheeky chap!
I'll chase him down with a well-aimed nap!

Banana peels slip, yet I'm on my way,
Through gardens of chaos, I prance and play.
The whisper of purpose? It's just my cat,
Ignoring my woes, and napping on that!

In mismatched moments, I decide to look,
For wisdom in chaos, in every nook.
A giggle here, a chuckle there,
Life's grand masterpiece, beyond compare!

Rebuilding from Ruins

In piles of papers and cereal crumbs,
I gather my thoughts like a troupe of drums.
A coffee spill here, a laughter there,
Turned rubble to castles with a whimsical flair.

A broken chair serves as my throne,
In the kingdom of chaos, I sit alone.
With duct tape and giggles, I make it right,
Building my dreams by the soft moonlight.

The dog steals my plans, what a furry thief,
But all's well in chaos, it's beyond belief.
I retrace my steps, with a hop and a skip,
In this maze of mayhem, there's magic to grip!

With laughter as my tool, I mend and I weave,
Turning mess into lesson; oh, you won't believe.
Each ruin a story, a burst of delight,
Creating my future, all out of sight!

Shattered Reflections

Mirrors cracked with a cheeky grin,
Reflect all my chaos, where do I begin?
A tangle of hair and mismatched socks,
I'm a jester of life, puzzling like blocks.

Every broken piece tells a tale, oh dear!
Like trying to herd cats, it's all quite clear.
With laughter as my compass, I wander and roam,
In this house of wonders, I still feel at home.

I juggle my dreams, they tumble, they fall,
Yet every silly slip is a dance at the ball.
A half-baked success? Who cares about that!
In a world full of chaos, I'm where it's at!

Shattered reflections, they sparkle and shine,
With a wink and a nudge, say, "Everything's fine!"
Between giggles and gasps, I stumble and play,
Finding joy in the chaos, come what may!

Cacophony of Purpose

A tune in my head, it's got rhythm and beat,
In the noise of the morning, my groove claims a seat.
From toasters to cars, it's a melody wild,
The cacophony sings, and I'm the delighted child.

Life's orchestra plays with a hint of absurd,
Each clattering pot is a note to be heard.
With mismatched percussion, I tap and I sway,
In this joyful chaos, I'm ready to play.

Groans of the fridge join a symphony grand,
As I dance with my lunch like it's all carefully planned.
With twirls and a twist, who knew it could be,
That purpose is playful, just look and you'll see!

So join me in laughter, let's waltz through the strife,
In chaotic cacophony, we savor this life.
With every blunder and song on repeat,
We find in the mayhem, a joy so sweet!

Serendipity in the Shuffle

In a world of wild mess, we trip on our feet,
The socks rarely match, yet we dance to the beat.
Coffee spills like confetti from a cup on the floor,
We laugh at the chaos, craving just a bit more.

A cat on the counter, a dog by the door,
Each day is a comedy, who could ask for more?
We bumble through moments, just chasing the sun,
With a wink and a grin, it's a riotous run.

Jumbled up plans, but so what, here we go!
Life's like a circus, and we're putting on a show.
With juggling of dreams, some break, but that's fine,
Each flop turns to laughter; it's all part of the line.

Through the mess of it all, smiles light up the day,
In the shuffle of life, we find our own way.
So here's to the flounder, the slip, and the dive,
In the heart of the shuffle, we truly feel alive!

A Dance in the Fray

Twist and turn, on the dance floor we sway,
Elbows bump, and toes get in the way.
In the rhythm of chaos, we spin and we jive,
Twirling through blunders, feeling so alive.

With partners all giggly, in mismatched attire,
We step on each other, but our hearts are on fire.
Who cares what's a misstep when laughter's the goal?
In the clumsiness, we discover our soul.

We might lose our balance on this wobbly spree,
But oh what a journey, just come dance with me.
Every twirl is a treasure, every trip a delight,
In this messy ballet, we dance through the night.

Chaos is charming, so let's spin till we fall,
With each silly misstep, we still stand tall.
In the fray of the dance, where confusion abounds,
We twirl with abandon, and joy knows no bounds!

Light in the Schism

In the crack of the chaos, a flicker appears,
Mismatched ideas, yet we chuckle at fears.
A riddle unraveled, though tangled it seems,
In the absurdity blooms the wildest of dreams.

With socks on our hands and hats on our feet,
We wander through mayhem, where nonsense is sweet.
Every blunder, a badge, every fall a good laugh,
As we navigate life's crooked old path.

Chaos is clever, like a dog in a cat's hat,
It winks at the trouble, invites us to chat.
We stumble through puzzles, all jumbled and bright,
Finding treasures in schisms, through our comical plight.

So here's to the sparks that shine through the mess,
In the struggle and giggles, we find our true zest.
Amidst all the chaos, be merry, don't fret,
There's light in the schism, just grab it, don't sweat!

Mosaic of Hope

Shattered pieces scattered, a puzzle in time,
With glue made of laughter, we'll sort out the grime.
A jigsaw of fumbles, with colors so bright,
We create a mosaic from the chaos of life.

Life's like a buffet, so much on the plate,
With forks full of whimsy, let's savor the fate.
Each weird little choice adds flavor and zest,
In this banquet of blunders, we're truly the best.

In the chaos of juggling our dreams and our woes,
We find that the laughter and joy never close.
With patches of sunshine, and sides of slapstick,
A tapestry woven from laughter's own trick.

So here's to the moments, the kooky and strange,
In the canvas of life, we embrace every change.
With mishaps united, we'll cheer and we'll cope,
In the artwork of chaos, we craft a great hope!

The Dance of Order and Mayhem

In a world where socks go rogue,
And spoons run marathons in the fog,
I waltz with chaos, feet a-misstep,
Spinning 'round like a clown on a log.

Juggling tasks like a circus ace,
With coffee spilling in this wild race,
Laughter echoes in my frantic chase,
As I trip over my own shoelace.

The cat joins in, with a grand pounce,
Caught off-guard, I stumble, then bounce!
In this frenzy, we frolic and flinch,
Learning to groove in the unexpected inch.

So let them dance, the lost and the free,
For in this mayhem, there's glee, you see?
We flip the script, and spin with delight,
Turning mistakes into confetti at night.

Beneath the Ruins

Beneath the rubble of dreams once bright,
I sift through laughs, holding on tight,
Amongst the chaos, I spot a grin,
As I step on a Lego, oh, the din!

Cracks in my plans, like a pie gone wrong,
Yet here I hum my silly song,
With every stumble, a chuckle is found,
In crumbled hopes, joy knows no bounds.

So raise a toast to the fallen bricks,
To life's little messes and funny tricks,
Each toppled tower a reason to cheer,
In this wild adventure, I hold dear.

Among the ruins, I learn to play,
In the silliness, I find my way,
For life's grand design is chaos in hues,
And laughter, my friend, is the best of views.

Seeds of Hope

Planting seeds in a garden of jest,
Watering dreams, I'm feeling blessed,
Among the weeds and gnarled twine,
Each sprout a giggle, oh so divine.

The squirrel steals my lunch with a flair,
Acting like it's a Broadway affair,
As I chase it, laughter fills the air,
In this wild dance, we make quite the pair.

Through dirt and chaos, the blooms arise,
With petals of joy, under bright blue skies,
I learn to embrace the silly, the wild,
In every stumble, I find the child.

Sprouting joy in a garden of fun,
Even as life just seems to run,
For what is chaos if not a stage,
Where laughter grows and joy's all the rage?

Tides of Meaning Amidst the Confusion

Riding the waves of a thought gone astray,
I paddle through puddles, come what may,
With rubber ducks as my trusty crew,
Singing off-key, just to break through.

The tide pulls back then crashes again,
I tumble and roll, but never in vain,
For every splash brings a giggle and cheer,
In this unpredictable realm, I hold dear.

Navigating life like a ship made of cheese,
Dodging the storms, my heart's filled with ease,
In the galley of chaos, I feast on the fun,
With a side of confusion, I'd never shun.

So let's ride these tides, with a wink and a grin,
Sway to the rhythm, let the chaos begin,
For laughter's the anchor, the sail, and the goal,
In the ocean of madness, it fills up my soul.

Lanterns in the Darkest Hours

In the depths of night, where shadows creep,
I stumble around, half-asleep,
Tripping on toys, oh, what a sight,
As I dance with the darkness, looking for light.

I wield a flashlight, my sword of zest,
In this epic quest, I'm truly blessed,
The monsters I meet, they giggle and play,
As we share our secrets in a curious way.

With lanterns of laughter, I light up the gloom,
Banishing fears, making room for the bloom,
For each chuckle, a spark ignites,
Dispelling the shadows, embracing the heights.

So here's to the night, and the mischief it brings,
To silly adventures and whimsical things,
In the darkest of hours, I'll dance and I'll sing,
With lanterns of humor, my heart takes wing.

The Soul's Revelation

In the midst of the mess, I search for my sock,
Hoping it's here, not on a neighbor's block.
Juggling my dreams while spilling my tea,
Who knew finding purpose was so messy for me?

Chasing my cat, he's off like a dart,
Paws up in laughter, he's stealing my heart.
With each little stumble, I giggle and sigh,
Looks like my path has a twisty sky-high!

A dance in the kitchen, I spill flour galore,
Creating a masterpiece, or maybe a war.
Life's recipe calls for a splash and a laugh,
Turns out my chaos is part of the craft!

So here's to the chaos, my silliness thrives,
Embracing the mess as I shuffle through lives.
From mismatched socks to the wild, free dance,
I've come to embrace this wild, crazy chance.

Casting Light in the Fog

Waking up slow, I can't find my key,
It's hiding somewhere, just laughing at me.
Fog in my brain, too thick to get by,
But that's where the fun is—who needs to comply?

Shortcut through life? I'll take it with flair,
Tangled in twinkly lights, I'm stuck, but I dare.
The path may be blurry, but watch me arrive,
Like a clown with a purpose, I'm ready to thrive.

With bright-colored dreams and mismatched parade,
I'm charting my course, even in disarray.
So sprinkle the joy like confetti of gold,
Chaos is where the best stories unfold!

I'll shine like a beacon amidst all the noise,
Dancing through life with my whimsical poise.
Each misstep a chance, let the laughter ignite,
In a world full of fog, I'll still be the light.

Resilience Finds Its Way

Woke in a tangle, my hair like a nest,
But who said that chaos can't look its best?
With coffee in hand and a spoon like a sword,
I battle the day with a giggle and word!

Stumbles and fumbles, my path looks a mess,
But laughter's my armor, I'm feeling quite blessed.
Life's a wild ride, like a rollercoaster,
Screaming through twists, yet I'm the lone toaster.

Monsters of doubt lurk behind every door,
I greet them with humor, then ask them for more.
Resilience is quirky, it makes me a star,
Charting a course that's absurd but bizarre!

So here's to the bumbles and laughter galore,
I'll dance through the chaos, forever explore.
In the midst of it all, I'm ready to play,
With a heart full of joy, I'll find my own way.

Life's Hidden Rhythms

Dancing in pajamas, I've lost track of time,
Hopscotch on pavement, or strolling in rhyme.
Waltzing with coffee, in slippers I glide,
Unruly and carefree, I'm a wild joyride!

The beat of the chaos rings loud in my ears,
A symphony crafted of giggles and cheers.
Finding the rhythm in splatters and spills,
Life's secret dance lives among all the thrills.

I trip through the day like a dancer offbeat,
But that's when the magic makes life feel complete.
So twirl through the mishaps, embrace every twist,
For harmony thrives where the chaos can't resist!

Each stumble's a note in this wild, crazy song,
In the symphony of life, we all dance along.
With laughter as tempo, let's jig through the fray,
For hidden in chaos, we find our own sway.

Embracing the Unknown

In a world where socks go stray,
I dance with dust, come what may,
My cat's my guide, he purrs so loud,
We'll conquer chaos, bold and proud.

Lost in the fridge, I seek a snack,
With leftover pizza, I'm on track,
A treasure map to lunch awaits,
Amidst the crumbs, we celebrate.

Winds may howl, the rain may whine,
I'll scribble doodles, call them divine,
Messy hair and mismatched shoes,
In this chaos, I choose to cruise.

With a splash of paint and goofy grace,
I'll paint my path, I'll find my space,
Life's a circus, laughter's the key,
Embracing the strange keeps me carefree.

The Search for North

I grabbed a compass, what a twist,
It points to coffee, I can't resist,
The map is scribbled, the route unclear,
Let's chase the snacks, my map's sincere.

The stars above are head-scratchers too,
One looks like fries, the other's a shoe,
I'll follow my gut, an adventurous ride,
With nachos and laughter right by my side.

Through parks of dog poop, we trudge along,
Each bump a note in our silly song,
Lost in the woods, my friend trips and laughs,
In this grand quest, let's take silly paths.

With every turn, a joke to unfurl,
Life's like my hair, a tangled swirl,
The north I seek might lead me astray,
But joy is my compass, come what may.

Awakening in the Storm

Raindrops tap-dance on my roof,
With each plop, I lose my poof,
I step outside, umbrella's broke,
Embrace the wet, it's no cruel joke.

A squirrel scurries, slips and slides,
In this downpour, he boldly hides,
I join the chaos, waddle and twirl,
Puddles become my splashy world.

The thunder claps, a sound disgrace,
I giggle and dance, it's quite the race,
Lightning flashing, a selfie moment,
Embracing the storm, my wet containment.

Through the puddles, I hop and skit,
With every splash, the world's a wit,
Raincoat? Nah, I'll wear my spree,
Awakening laughter, just wild and free.

Hues of Resilience

Crayons scattered, colors galore,
With wobbly lines, I'll never bore,
A masterpiece born from clumsy hands,
In this vibrant chaos, my spirit stands.

Life spills paint, it's messy and bright,
Splashes of joy in the dead of night,
With every drip, I find my tune,
A dancing palette beneath the moon.

Here's to the moments, both shaky and fun,
Mixing up colors until we're done,
A canvas of chaos, I proudly boast,
I'll laugh with the hues that I cherish most.

Brush in hand, I twirl and play,
With every stroke, I'll pave the way,
In resilience' arms, I shout and cheer,
In this colorful chaos, I've found my sphere.

Finding Harmony in Dissonant Tunes

When life's a wacky, wild parade,
You'll find your rhythm, don't be afraid.
In the cacophony, dances arise,
Even the clumsy can win the prize.

So tap your feet to the offbeat sound,
See how the silly can be profound.
A jig in the kitchen, a twist in the hall,
Dancing with chaos, you'll have a ball.

Mix socks for shoes, wear a hat that's too wide,
Join in the madness, embrace every ride.
With laughter and tunes that are strangely in sync,
You'll discover the joy in each crazy wink.

From bewildering beats, let your heart smile,
The wobbly steps make it all worth the while.
In this orchestra playing out in the streets,
Find harmony nestled in quirky retreats.

The Journey Beyond the Storm

Kites in the wind, we're ready to fly,
Dodging the raindrops, under a bright sky.
Each gust of trouble may tug at our seams,
Yet we'll navigate through with whimsical dreams.

Puddles like mirrors, we stomp and we splash,
Laughing and dodging in a joyful dash.
With umbrellas turned inside out, we spin,
Making a game of the storm we're in.

The thunder's a drum that keeps our hearts bold,
Lightning flash-writes stories yet to be told.
As rain turns to laughter, what a delight!
We'll find our way home, just follow the light.

So let's shout and dance through the storm so bright,
Navigating chaos with sheer delight.
With bubbly spirits and whimsical cheers,
We'll weather the journey, dismiss all our fears.

Radiance from Relentless Winds

Whirling and twirling, the leaves take flight,
Dancing with fervor in the glowing light.
The wind howls a tune, raucous yet clear,
Guiding our giggles far and near.

So grab your hat, let's plan a wild chase,
For in every gust, there's laughter to brace.
With hair like a tumbleweed, (oh what a sight!),
We'll find our spark in this breezy delight.

Chasing our dreams down the twisty lane,
Even the oddest can dance in the rain.
For in gusty chaos, our hearts find their song,
Swinging with humor as we whirl along.

Radiate joy, let your spirit unfurl,
In the breeziest chaos, let your sense twirl.
For every gust that seems to confound,
Can lead us to laughter, where love will surround.

Chasing Shadows Towards the Light

Under the moon, where shadows play games,
We sprint through the park, with giggles, not names.
For every dark corner, there's laughter to find,
In the chase of the shadows, we're all intertwined.

Hiding behind trees, we leap and we bound,
Those giggly echoes are the best kind of sound.
With every wild flicker that dances in sight,
We'll chase the odd shadows 'til the dawn's light.

Flashlight in hand, our courage will soar,
As shadows turn silly, we'll ask them for more.
So let's play our games with glee on our face,
For even in darkness, we'll find our own place.

With hearts open wide, and a playful delight,
We'll dance with the shadows till morning is bright.
In this whimsical world, where chaos has charm,
We'll find all the magic, safe and warm.

Mapping the Lost

The map is upside-down, what a sight!
I swear I was headed the right way, just last night.
With a sandwich in hand and a cat on my lap,
I wonder if the GPS might need a nap.

The stars have a chuckle, they twinkle and wink,
"Lost again, dear friend? Maybe rethink!"
The signs point the wrong way, but that's quite alright,
I'll follow the ice cream truck, just for a bite.

A compass is spinning, it's in a dance,
I've got two left feet, but I might take a chance.
With laughter as fuel, I'll adventure bold,
Even misadventures are treasures to hold.

So here's my map, it scribbles and flaps,
Filled with doodles and plans that get into mishaps.
I'll wander these paths where the oddballs convene,
Contemplating life, with a side of ice cream.

Embracing the Whirlwind

Caught in a whirlwind, oh what fun!
It tossed my hat, and it stole my bun.
I giggle and twirl, like a leaf on the way,
This tempest of laughter is here to stay.

Chasing the chaos, I trip on my shoe,
A tumble, a roll, hey, how do you do?
The world is a circus, I'm part of the show,
With popcorn and cotton candy, let's go-go-go!

A jester's grin spreads wide on my face,
I dance with the wind, in this frantic race.
The clouds might just party, in a stormy ballet,
We spin on our heels, shake worries away.

So bring on the whirlwinds, I'll spin like a top,
In the heart of the madness, I'll never stop.
With a wink and a laugh, I embrace every twist,
As if each little chaos was carefully missed.

In the Midst of the Tempest

In the midst of the tempest, I juggle a pie,
The sky's throwing tantrums, oh me, oh my!
With rain in my face, I try not to slip,
While ducks take flight on my unplanned trip.

A lighthouse is blinking, "What's your next move?"
I can't read the signs, but I've got the groove.
On seas filled with jelly, I steer with a grin,
I'll surf on the chaos, let the fun begin!

The thunder is roaring, a grumpy old man,
But I'll dance in the storm, slapstick is the plan.
Each gust teaches lessons wrapped in a joke,
As I sail through the madness, I give life a poke.

Umbrella inverted, a clown at the helm,
I'll skip through this tempest, I'll take back my realm.
With laughter as oars, I'll sail wide and free,
Finding joy in the chaos, that's the key!

The Pulse of Perseverance

With a bounce in my step, I leap over the muck,
Each slip and each slide is just plain good luck.
Through puddles and chaos, I'll dance and I'll sway,
My heart's got a rhythm, come join in the play.

A pogo stick daydream, I hop to the beat,
Dodging the raindrops that fall on my feet.
With a grin on my face, I'm a bobblehead king,
In the pulse of this madness, I've found my zing.

I'll juggle the chaos like a circus act,
Balancing whimsy, with courage intact.
Life may throw curveballs, but I won't despair,
I'll wear a big smile, and twirl through the air.

So here's to the chaos, let's give it a shout,
Each stumble and fumble is what life's about.
With laughter as fuel, I'll move to the sound,
In the pulse of this mayhem, purpose is found.

Reflections in a Turbulent Sea

Waves crash, I splash, oh what a sight,
My boat's a teacup in stormy fright.
With a rubber duck as my trusty guide,
I'll sail through the chaos, enjoy the ride.

Seagulls laugh as I drift along,
My compass is jammed, but hey, what's wrong?
I toss a fish back and shout with glee,
Who knew lost at sea could feel so free?

Drenched in the chaos, my spirit lifts,
Each wave a reminder, the ocean gifts.
I dance on deck, though I might fall down,
The chaos is here, but so is my crown.

So here's to the wild tides that spin and twirl,
I'll drink my coffee, let the chaos unfurl.
For in this mad swirl, there's joy to be found,
In each splash and each giggle, life knows no bound.

Chasing Clarity Through Dissonance

A symphony plays, but it's all out of tune,
Like cats on a rooftop singing to the moon.
I sing along, with no sense of fear,
Mistaking the chaos for music so clear.

Horns blare and the drums beat at odd times,
Each sound a riddle, though none make sense rhymes.
Yet in this cacophony, a rhythm does bloom,
A dance of confusion, let's brighten the gloom.

I've got maracas, a tambourine too,
Each note a giggle, puns that ensue.
Do I jump right or left with my wild guitar?
In this misfit parade, let's all be a star!

So grab your partner, and let's misstep,
In the dissonance, we find our pep.
For when life is a bungle, a laugh is the key,
To chase down the clarity and dance wild and free.

Echoes of Serenity Within the Noise

In a world blaring louder than my best friend's snore,
I search for the quiet behind the uproar.
My zen is a hamster on a spinning wheel,
Trying to meditate, but losing appeal.

The traffic's a concert, I'm stuck in the queue,
A dance of my own, as the cars pass through.
With headphones blaring tunes from a decade past,
I smile at the chaos, hoping it won't last.

The coffee shop's buzzing like bees on a spree,
Yet I sip my latte, so fancy and free.
For within all the noise, a moment does spark,
It's the laughter of strangers that lights up the dark.

So here's to the echoes that burst through the fray,
I'll laugh at the mess as I seize the day.
For in every cacophony, joy finds a voice,
And we learn through the clamor to dance and rejoice.

A Compass in Fragmented Skies

The clouds are all lost, floating here and there,
My compass is spinning, with nary a care.
A sandwich in hand serves as my control,
As I navigate life, playing out my role.

My GPS talks in riddles and rhymes,
"Turn left at the traffic, it's a Fisher-Price climb!"
Yet I chuckle along, enjoying the jest,
For every wrong turn is a well-earned quest.

So up in the sky, where the birds make their plans,
I spread out my map with peanut butter hands.
They squawk at my antics, join in the fun,
Finding direction when there's nowhere to run.

So here's to the wayward and ample delight,
In fragmented skies, let's just take flight.
For laughter is compass, come rain or come shine,
In the chaos of clouds, we all intertwine.

Beneath the Storm's Veil

In puddles I dance, oh what a sight,
My umbrella flips, it takes flight!
Raindrops ticking, a playful choir,
Who knew chaos could spark such fire?

Lost keys and muddy shoes at my feet,
A treasure map grid for snacks to eat!
Between the thunder, my mind does sway,
Finding joy in folly, it's my own way!

Threads of Meaning

Tangled yarn, oh where to start?
Knots of wisdom tug at my heart.
A sweater's worth of laughter and tears,
Crafting my life through giggles and fears.

Each stitch a story, each loop a laugh,
I knit my dreams on a wobbly path.
When the thread snaps, I shrug and grin,
Chaos reigns, let the knitting begin!

Navigating the Noise

With honks and clatter, it's quite a strain,
I strut through traffic, like it's a game.
The sirens wail, a curtsy, I bow,
In the midst of madness, I wonder how?

A parade of chaos, but I'm the star,
Juggling tasks in a wacky bazaar.
I ride the waves of clamor and din,
Amidst the frenzy, let the fun begin!

Echoes of Clarity

In the rabbit hole, I tumble and trip,
Searching for wisdom with a comic flip.
Echoes of laughter ring through the air,
In a world of nonsense, I'm learning to care.

With each twist and turn, I find my way,
Dodging the chaos, I'm here to play.
With giggles and sighs, a roadmap is drawn,
In the heart of confusion, I dance 'til dawn!

The Fire Within

In a world of socks that never match,
I seek a fiery dance, not a boring batch.
Like a chef with spices, I stir up plight,
Cooking chaos with laughter, a gourmet delight.

When mishaps tumble like a bear on skis,
I giggle at the mess with utmost ease.
For every spilled drink, a toast to the fates,
Life's a wild party, and I'm on the plates.

So let the flames rise, I'll fan them with glee,
Turn down the chaos and crank the spree.
With a wink and a grin, I embrace the heat,
For in this weird dance, life's a savory treat.

Here's to the blunders, the laughter, the show,
Through tangled up hair and a misfit bow.
With spirit unbroken, I'll rise from the din,
Forever igniting the fire within.

Illuminating Shadows

In the alley of shadows, a light does prance,
Playing hide and seek with a goofy dance.
Ghosts of my worries, they wiggle and sway,
Who knew being lost could be such a play?

With a flashlight that's blue and a pizza slice,
I navigate chaos, oh isn't it nice?
The shadows keep laughing, I join in too,
We're a raucous team in a costume review.

Each corner I turn, a bestseller plot,
With tangled-up yarn and a polka-dot spot.
I juggle my fears like a clown on a thread,
Sipping up giggles, nerves left for dead.

So cheers to the dance, to the chaos and cheer,
In this circus of life, I'll steer with a sneer.
For what seems a mess is a sparkly show,
Illuminating shadows where wild dreams flow.

The Bridge Over Troubled Waters

I built a bridge made of wobbly logs,
To cross over waters that bubble like frogs.
With a splash and a giggle, I take to the air,
As ducks quack in rhythm, life's joys to declare.

Each step a dance, a tightrope of fun,
As the waters below bubble, the chaos begun.
With a grin and a wiggle, I leap to the safe,
Laughing at stumbles, for joy is my waif.

What is a bridge without a little sway?
A plunge into water? No way, not today!
My bridge is a trampoline, bouncy and bright,
Where laughter's the anchor, I take off in flight.

So here's to the journey, the splashes and quirks,
Through troubled waters, I'll dance, do the works.
With buoyant reminders that fun is the key,
This bridge leads to laughter, sweet blasphemy.

A Tapestry of Trials

Woven in threads of an oddball's delight,
A tapestry sparkles with chaos in sight.
Each stitch a mishap, each color a laugh,
A fabric of folly, a whimsical path.

With socks on my hands and a hat on my feet,
I weave through the struggles, make failure my beat.
The more I trip over, the brighter I glow,
In this crazy quilt, I'm the star of the show.

Life's tapestry rustles with playful surprise,
Knots in the fabric become joyful ties.
For every frayed edge, there's a story to tell,
In this wacky adventure, I'm doing quite well.

So raise up a glass to the fabric of fate,
Embrace all the trials, just don't hesitate.
With laughter entwined in each fiber and hue,
My tapestry's chaos is a dream come true.

When the World is Unraveled

When socks run amok and the cat steals the toast,
I ponder my plans and wonder the most.
The coffee spills over, the dog chews my shoe,
Life's little chaos feels like a zoo.

Grocery lists vanish like socks in the wash,
And I'm left to scramble, my brain in a froth.
I search for a reason in this merry mess,
Yet chuckles arise, my heart beats, no stress.

The timing of traffic, an endless delay,
Makes me ponder if chaos is here just to play.
But with every misstep, I start to discern,
That laughter's the compass, life's twists make me learn.

So here's to the chaos, the slip-ups of fate,
Each tumble a tickle, no reason to wait.
For in this wild dance, the fun's just begun,
With every odd turn, I find I have won.

The Heart's Coordinates

Like a compass gone wild, spinning left, then to right,
My heart seeks direction in the midst of the night.
Maps tangled in laughter, where should I go?
With every mishap, my journey's aglow.

In coffee shop corners, a cloud of debate,
I chuckle at questions that pile up like fate.
The answers escape, just like birds from the tree,
But who cares for details when it's fun, we agree!

A GPS glitch in the midst of my drive,
Leads me to places I've never arrived.
But joy finds me always, in the maps that I trace,
With laughter taped firmly to all of my grace.

So let's toast to the wander, the sidesteps, the slips,
To tangled-up journeys with twists on our trips.
For the heart, uncoiled, like a kite in the breeze,
Discovers its path with giggles and ease.

Harmony from Dissonance

My socks sing the blues, mismatched in a row,
The kettle is whistling a sharp, wheezy flow.
Instruments clatter, the dog finds a bone,
Yet harmony flickers in chaos alone.

As I dance with the dishes, the forks make a beat,
The rhythm of chaos is wonderfully sweet.
The laundry's a symphony of colors and grime,
And I hum along to its off-key rhyme.

With each dish I tumble, a song starts to grow,
From the laughter that echoes, my spirit will flow.
The winds of confusion blow wildly around,
Yet in the disarray, I'm happily found.

So here's to the chaos, the tunes that it brings,
To finding my groove where laughter still sings.
In every mishap, a melody plays,
Chaotic orchestra, I cherish your ways.

Embracing the Whirlwind

In a whirlwind of feathers and giggles galore,
I brace for the chaos that's knocking at my door.
The wind picks up pillows, the cat zooms right by,
Life's comic tornado, oh my, look at it fly!

I chase after moments where sanity slips,
In the dance of confusion, I'm taking wild trips.
With half of my sandwich jammed in my hair,
It's hard to feel frantic when laughter is there.

I juggle my thoughts like a clown at a show,
With one shoe on my foot and a mystery toe.
The whirlwind may toss me like leaves in the fall,
But the fun of the chaos is the best part of all.

So let's revel in madness, the twists, and the spins,
Where joy is the prize, and the silliness wins.
For in this grand whirlwind of life's grand charade,
I find every joy in the games that we've played.

Voices of Wisdom in the Clamor

In a world that spins with noise,
Wisdom hides, it plays with toys.
Chasing squirrels and laughing loud,
Finding peace amidst the crowd.

Juggling tasks like clumsy clowns,
Wearing mismatched shoes and frowns.
A wise old sage in a bright red coat,
Sings his rhymes like a singing goat.

Through the chatter, one can glean,
Life's a circus, not a machine.
Taking a break from all the fuss,
Is the secret to avoiding the bus.

When the chaos seems to reign,
Dance with dogs, let go of pain.
In the madness, find a rhythm,
Hum along, create your own hymn.

Emerging from the Chaos' Embrace

In a twisty world of tangled strings,
I wrestle with all kinds of things.
Finding socks that never match,
It's a chaotic life, a funny scratch.

Amidst the laughter and the heat,
I trip on toys, shout out defeat.
Yet in the mayhem, joy still thrives,
Oh, the shenanigans of our lives!

I danced with chaos, held it tight,
Fell off a chair, what a silly sight!
But from the tumble and the fall,
A goofy grin is what I haul.

Through the whirl, the giggles bloom,
In the mess, there's always room.
For laughter's the balm, a joyful trace,
Emerging strong from chaos' embrace.

The Art of Stillness in Motion

In a busy café where teacups clink,
Finding stillness is key, don't you think?
I sip my brew, then spill it wide,
As I laugh at the mess, it's my joyride.

While the world rushes, I take my time,
Counting spoons, I make them rhyme.
In this chaos, I find my way,
Wobbling like a duck, I'll stay.

Life's a dance of coffee beans,
Waltzing wildly in my dreams.
Every spill, a graceful turn,
In the chaos, I still learn.

With every sip, the chaos fades,
As I craft my own charades.
Stillness found in motion's swirl,
Creates a funny, quirky whirl.

Blossoms Rising from the Ashes

From the flames of toast, I found a snack,
A burnt delight, oh, what a knack!
In the kitchen chaos, I embrace,
The scent of smoke, a warming grace.

Juggling eggs, I'm on the brink,
The floor's a mess, but I don't think.
In laughter, the burnt bread finds its way,
Join the party; we'll dance today.

Like flowers sprouting in concrete cracks,
Life's a comedy; just relax.
Through the craziness, I see the blooms,
In a wild world, even chaos zooms.

Rising from mishaps, oh, what a sight,
Every folly turns the day bright.
With every chuckle, we'll splash and sway,
Blossoms thrive in their own quirky play.

Whispers Among the Storm

In the gusts, my hat takes flight,
Chasing it feels so right,
Umbrellas do a tango dance,
While I stumble like a prance.

Raindrops play a silly tune,
Jumping puddles 'neath the moon,
Chaos spins a wobbly waltz,
Guess who's fumbling? It's my faults!

Lightning flashes, dogs all bark,
I juggle thoughts, missed my mark,
But in this mess, I find a way,
To laugh and dance through disarray.

In the chaos, joy alights,
Tickled funny by the sights,
With every storm that comes to play,
I wear my smile, come what may.

In the Eye of Uncertainty

Spinning circles 'round my brain,
Like a cat that's lost its lane,
Dodging questions like a pro,
Why do I feel such a glow?

The winds may howl, the skies may drip,
I dance, I twirl, and take a sip,
Tea's too hot, but I just jest,
This twist is quite a fun-filled test!

Clouds above wear silly hats,
As I weave, just like the cats,
Chasing colors swirling 'round,
In this madness, joy I've found.

Chaos spins, my laughter grows,
Between each doubt, a spark just shows,
So here I am, in this odd spree,
Laughing madly, wild, and free!

Threads of Light in the Shadows

In the dim, where giggles creep,
Socks go missing, who's to keep?
Bumbling fools beneath the bed,
Picking fights with dusty dread.

Candles flicker, shadows play,
I catch a laugh that skips away,
Light twirls in a twisted race,
Under chaos, I find my space.

Mismatched shoes on wobbly feet,
Giggling as I dare compete,
Life's a circus, oh, what fun!
In the fray, I've already won.

Through the dark, a silly jest,
In the mess, I feel the best,
With every slip and slide I take,
I weave the joy; I feel awake!

Navigating the Tempest's Heart

Here I sail from tea to toast,
In stormy seas, I love the most,
With a spoon as my trusty oar,
Who needs sense when I can explore?

Clouds are grumpy, winds are wild,
But I'm a carefree, chaos child,
Waves may crash, but I just cheer,
For every splash, a giggle near.

Maps? Who needs that kind of tool?
I draw my lines, just play the fool,
"Where to now?" I grin and shrug,
Navigating chaos with a hug.

So here's to storms that swirl and spin,
With joy, I dive, let the fun begin,
In the whirlwind, my heart takes part,
Finding rhythm in the tempest's heart.

Embracing the Turbulent Flow

Life's a dance without a beat,
We stumble, trip, and laugh in heat.
With socks that never seem to match,
We ride the waves, no need to scratch.

In storms we twirl, a silly sight,
Like rubber ducks in wild moonlight.
We sip our tea while chaos reigns,
Then burst out loud, ignoring pains.

With rumbling tummies, we make a pact,
To juggle dreams and keep on track.
In all the mess, we find the glue,
And paint our lives in shades of blue.

So let it whirl, this silly ride,
We'll laugh and giggle side by side.
In tangled yarns, our lives unfurl,
Embracing all, we do a twirl.

Chaos to Clarity

In the circus of unkempt hair,
We juggle laughter, dance with flair.
Between the pies that go awry,
We piece together dreams that fly.

When socks go missing in the wash,
We sit and think, then laugh with posh.
With every slip, we learn the way,
With spilled coffee, we'll seize the day.

Confetti falls, the cat runs by,
We miss the mess but still we try.
With every laugh, we find a road,
In chaos's grip, we drop the load.

So as we dance on life's high wire,
We twirl and leap and never tire.
In tangled turns, we see it clear,
That in the mess, we shed a tear.

Stitches of the Soul

With needle and thread, we patch the night,
Stitching smiles with all our might.
In a quilt of dreams, with colors bright,
We sew our tales, a funny sight.

The cat's a seamstress, eyes in glee,
As yarn goes flying, oh woe is me!
Each knot a giggle, each loop a cheer,
In every slip, our hearts grow near.

As socks conspire to hide away,
We forge ahead, come what may.
With every stitch, a lesson learned,
In chaotic hands, our hearts still yearn.

So here's our fabric, full of life,
In tussles and giggles, we conquer strife.
With stitches woven, tales to tell,
In this great fabric, we all dwell.

Winds of Change

When winds of whimsy blow our way,
We gather round for fun and play.
With hats askew and shoes untied,
We sail through storms, our faces wide.

The leaves may dance; we twirl and spin,
In every gust, new laughs begin.
With every flip of fate's own page,
We chuckle loud, embrace the stage.

With lemonade spilled and cake in face,
We find the joy in every space.
The chaos swirls, we laugh and cheer,
With every turn, it's crystal clear.

So let the winds bring what they will,
We're armed with laughter, strong and still.
In breezy folly, we take our stance,
In whirlwinds wild, we learn to dance.

www.ingramcontent.com/pod-product-compliance
Lightning Source LLC
Chambersburg PA
CBHW051701160426
43209CB00004B/984